THE
Archive Photographs
SERIES

RICHMOND AND KEW

The Steps, Richmond c. 1907 between Tower House on the left and Richmond Bridge. On The Steps the children behind are staring at the camera while a man sits posing by the boat. The camera just catches the movement of the woman with the dog.

THE
Archive Photographs
SERIES

RICHMOND
AND KEW

Compiled by
Richard Essen

CHALFORD

First published 1995
Copyright © Richard Essen, 1995

The Chalford Publishing Company
St Mary's Mill, Chalford,
Stroud, Gloucestershire, GL6 8NX

ISBN 0 7524 0145 9

Typesetting and origination by
The Chalford Publishing Company
Printed in Great Britain by
Redwood Books, Trowbridge

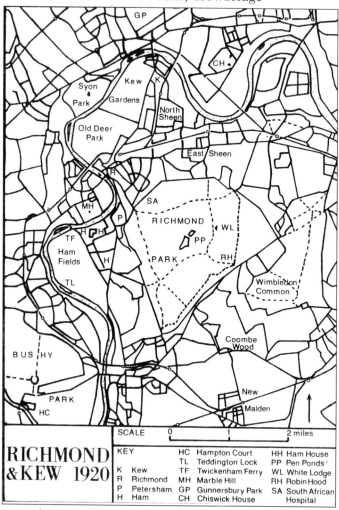

A map based upon the 1974 Ordnance Survey 1: 50,000 map with the permission of the Controller of H.M.S.O. (c) Crown Copyright.

Contents

Richmond Station, British Rail, 1971, with neon lights on the island in the middle of the road and an Evening Standard delivery van outside the station. On the far left is Westminster House and on the far right Chancellors, chartered surveyors and estate agents in Richmond since the 1890s.

Acknowledgements

Thanks are due to the British Architectural Library, RIBA, London, Lens of Sutton, the London Transport Museum, Mayfair Cards of London, the Museum of Richmond and the Local Studies Library, the National Railway Museum, and the Ordnance Survey.

Most of the books used have been published recently and so have been listed by area and author rather than date. On Richmond, works include John Cloake's *Richmond in old photographs* (1990), *The Growth of Richmond* (1993) and *Richmond Past* (1994), and Tim Sherwood's *The Railways of Richmond Upon Thames*. Also *Richmond, Surrey as it was* (1992) by The Historical and Archaeological Section of the Richmond Society.

On Richmond Park, C.L. Collenette's *A History of Richmond Park* (1971) and Michael Baxter-Brown's *Richmond Park, the history of a Royal Deer Park*. On Kew, G.E. Cassidy's *Kew as it was* and David Broomfield's *The Story of Kew* (1992) and *Kew Past* (1994). On Kew Gardens, Gwilym Lewis' *Postcards from Kew* (1989) and Johnathan Riddell and William T. Stearn's *By Underground to Kew* (1994). On Ham and Petersham, James Green and Silvia Greenwood's *Ham and Petersham as it was* (1992). On Chiswick, Carolyn and Peter Hammond's *Chiswick* in the Old Photographs Series (1994). Finally, general books used include *Arthur Mee's Surrey* (1955) by Arthur Mee, and B.K. Cooper's *Southern Railway Handbook* (1983).

Introduction

Richmond and Kew, sitting in a promontory of the River Thames to the west of London, attracted royalty early. This in turn attracted the business or middle classes and when the railways opened up the area a Victorian suburb was quickly built in the 1890s. This set Richmond and Kew out from other Surrey Boroughs because most were further away from London and had to wait until the thirties before they received housing on the same scale as Richmond in the 1890s. It is this history, from 1890 to 1965, which is set out in five chapters covering the Victorian and Edwardian (Chapter 1), the First World War (Chapter 2), the Twenties and Thirties (Chapter 3), the Second World War (Chapter 4), and the Fifties and Sixties (Chapter 5).

Richmond and Kew (Chapter 1) are bordered by the River Thames which has probably influenced their shape. The area was originally called Shene meaning 'a place of shelter' and Kayho which probably means 'the landing place on the promontory'. They attracted royalty both on the alluvial flood plains at Shene Palace and on the London clay of Richmond Park. In 1501 King Henry VII re-named Shene Palace after Richmond, his earldom in Yorkshire. The royal association was continued by the Hanoverian kings at Kew Palace around which Kew Gardens were designed. In the nineteenth century Richmond too became a fashionable resort encouraging development around the Greens at Richmond, Ham and Kew typifying 'Village London'. The railways, drawn by this fashionable area, encouraged the early development of housing which doubled the population from 10,962 in 1861 to 19,066 in 1881.

The new status as a Victorian suburb was confirmed in the formation of the Borough of Richmond by Royal Charter on 16 July 1890. It not only expressed its civic pride in public buildings but also helped in the development of both middle and working class estates. The public buildings included the Duchess of Teck memorial (1891), the Town Hall (1893), Richmond Lock Bridge (1894), the County School for boys (1895), Richmond Theatre (1899), Kew Bridge (1903), Darell Road School (1906), the County Secondary School for girls, Richmond (1908) and Gainsborough Secondary School (1912–13). The new estates included middle class houses at Kew and on the eastern slopes of Richmond Hill, and working class housing along the railway lines including the Manor Grove estate (1894) built under the 1890 Housing of the Working Classes Act.

By the Edwardian reign this new centre was fed by extensions to the motor bus routes bringing new workers to the houses and weekend visitors to the river and the new parks. The Borough of Richmond did not want trams or trolleybuses so it was reliant on the motor bus since the railways had to go around Richmond Park by the Kingston loop. Domestic servants were brought in along two new bus routes, the General's 37 providing a west-east link between Richmond and Peckham, and the General's 73 providing a north-south link between Richmond and Stoke Newington. Kew was linked by a General route 27 to Highgate. The same routes with extensions were used at weekends for day trippers coming for the rowing, punting, river excursions and walks. Richmond town centre became full of tea shops to cater for the visitors. It had space for this role though as it was not a market town because Kingston had market rights within a seven-mile radius so it was always more a social centre than an economic one.

Building was only held up by the First World War (Chapter 2), when Richmond Park was used as a training camp and work switched to war production (The Whitehead Aircraft Company). In Richmond Park there were camps at the Roehampton Paddocks used by a London Scottish Regiment in 1915 and a South African Hospital. There were Red Cross hospitals at the Green, the Star and Garter, and Grove Road Hospital.

In the twenties and thirties (Chapter 3) the war was commemorated by the red brick Star and Garter Home for Disabled Servicemen (1924) and the re-siting of the Poppy Factory in Richmond (1925). After the war the River Thames, which borders most of the boundaries of the borough, continued to be used for entertainment with punts, row boats, pleasure cruises and strolls by the river or in the riverside parks. At Kew the Gardens drew many visitors encouraged by innovative London Transport posters. At both Richmond and Kew, in addition to boat yards, hotels and tea houses grew up around the Park and Gardens. The area has also been prone to flooding which is why the lock was built in 1894 as a flood defence to manage the water supply. In 1928 however the defences were breached and 500 houses were flooded at Kew. The benefits of the river, though, have included good pasture land on the floodplains for the cows which supported local dairies. The sports have also been river-based with an active Richmond canoe club. Other land based sports have had an upper class following with running (the Ranelagh Harriers) and shooting (the Petersham Rifle Club) in Petersham and rugby at Richmond as internationals developed there first before moving to Twickenham. London Scottish and London Welsh are still located in Richmond.

The 1890s estates were finished off after the war and although the urban district of Ham was added in 1933, there was not the same scale of thirties housebuilding as other Surrey boroughs because so much had been built in the 1890s. Additions were limited to the road and railway infrastructure with the building of the Great Chertsey Road and bridges (1928–33) and stations at North Sheen and Richmond. Other additions can be identified by the Art Deco architecture found on Richmond Odeon (1930), the British Legion Poppy Factory (1933), Richmond station (1937), and The Ritz cinema (1938).

During the Second World War (Chapter 4), as early as September 1938 air raid shelters were built on Richmond and Kew Greens. Most civil defence measures were temporary, though. At Kew the Ministry of Labour buildings and the Occupation Road that ran beside the railway were requisitioned and used by the RAF, US troops, and Italian POWs. A Home Guard was formed and a morale boosting procession of civil defence organisations was made through Richmond during April 1941. Richmond Park and Kew Green were used over to cultivate crops and the Park was once again used for war training. Kew also became a host to refugee families, since the heavy bombing when planes heading for the Great West Road or London dropped their bombs early, meant some homes were evacuated.

In the fifties and sixties (Chapter 5) while Richmond rebuilt war damage other outer London boroughs finished off pre-war estates and expanded their populations. The result was that the population of Richmond had only increased by about 4,000 from 37,797 in 1931 to 41,945 in 1951. This was reflected in 1965 when Barnes and Twickenham were added to form the London Borough of Richmond Upon Thames and the Town Hall became a Museum of the Borough of Richmond's past.

One
Victorian and Edwardian

THE THAMES RICHMOND

The River Thames at Richmond, c. 1914, showing its use during the Edwardian era for pleasure. It is a good picture to start with since the Borough is bounded by the river which has probably been the major influence on its shape.

The gateway to the courtyard of Richmond Palace, c. 1905, was the first of the royal palaces to be built on the flood plains overlooking the river in 1500. The gate-house and Wardrobe Court are all that remain of the Tudor Palace.

The King's Breakfast Room at Kew Palace was built in 1631 as the Dutch House and bought by King George III in 1781 as an annexe to his main residence the White House until it was demolished in 1802. When King George moved to Windsor Queen Charlotte continued to live at Kew Palace until 1818.

The Queen's Cottage, c. 1908. King George III had this built for Queen Charlotte, probably in the 1770s. It was given with 37 acres of woodlands to the Gardens as a Diamond Jubilee gift by Queen Victoria in 1897.

White Lodge, Richmond Park, *c.* 1906, was built 1727–9 for George I and became a home for Lord Sidmouth, the park ranger, in 1804, and briefly for Queen Victoria and King Edward VII. It became the home of the Duke and Duchess of Teck in 1869 and the future King Edward VIII was born here in 1894. The Duchess of Teck died here on 27 October 1897 and the Duke in 1899.

Buccleuch House was built 1761–2 and inherited by the Duke of Buccleuch. It was sold in 1887 by the Richmond Vestry to Sir J. Whittaker-Ellis, who represented the Kingston Division in Parliament. He entertained the Duke and Duchess of Teck and King George V and Queen Mary (when Duke and Duchess of York) at the House.

Ham House, *c*. 1905. The house forms the nucleus around which Ham is built. It was first built in 1610 in an H-plan and was bought by William Murray, the first Earl of Dysart, about 1630 who rebuilt the interior. His daughter the Countess of Dysart and her husband, the Duke of Lauderdale, modified it into a rectangle (1672–4).

PETERSHAM LODGE.

Petersham Lodge, *c*. 1906. River Lane was built *c*. 1740 and bought by Sir Max Waechter, who in June 1902 presented the freehold to the Richmond Corporation for the preservation of the view from Richmond Hill.

All Saints', Bute Avenue, Petersham, c. 1909, was built 1907–08 in a Romanesque style out of proportion to the population it was serving, with a 108 feet high tower. Mrs Lionel Warde, who had bought the Bute House estate, was waiting for an expected increase in the population which never took place.

Petersham Road, *c.* 1900, showing the walls around Richmond Park and the Bute House gates which were an entrance to it.

St Peter's Church, Petersham, *c.* 1905, is part of the earliest area of Petersham with a thirteenth-century chancel. The south transept and galleries were added in 1840. It is next to Petersham House and is rather modest when compared with All Saints'.

A North London Railway poster for the company which began operating to Richmond via Barnes in 1853 and via Kew Gardens in 1869. The poster shows its distinctive engines finished in a black livery and offers an open air route to Broad Street which was the London terminus for this company opened in 1865. Broad Street was only recently demolished in 1987. (National Railway Museum)

A Metropolitan Railway engine at the New Richmond Station platform going to Aldgate. The District began operating to Mansion House on 1 June 1877 and the Metropolitan to Aldgate from 1 October 1877. The Metropolitan service lasted until 1906 making the District the sole Underground company running to Richmond after the Underground Group was formed in 1908. (Lens of Sutton)

A London and South Western Railway advert of 1904 advertising its routes to the South West of England. In the years 1877–1906, five railway companies, the District, Great Western, London and South Western, Metropolitan and North London Railways, operated from Richmond.

Richmond Station *c*. 1906 consisted of two stations, Old (1848) and New (1869). The through London and South Western Railway lines on the left running from Waterloo to Windsor lead to the Old station. In 1906 the New station on the right was a terminus for the London and South Western, District, and North London Railways.

Richmond Station, *c*. 1906. The London and South Western Railway Class T1 steam engine no. 75 on the right occupies the District Railway platforms which were electrified on 1 August 1905. On the right of this is the North London Railway platform to Broad Street. The layout is a reverse of the position occupied by District and North London trains today. (Lens of Sutton)

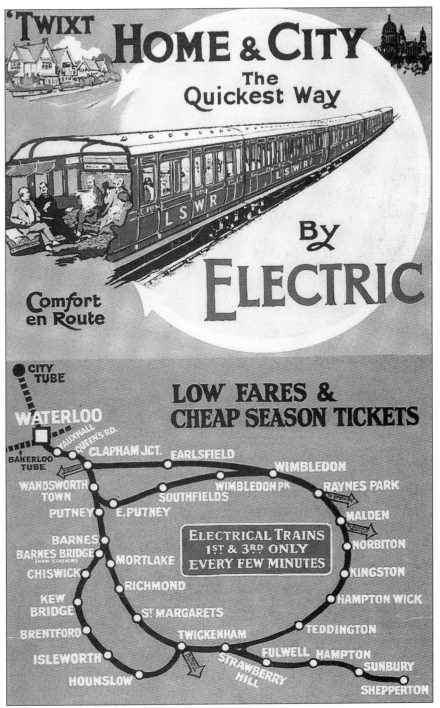

A London and South Western Railway advert for electric trains, 1916, showing the Kingston and Hounslow loops electrified on 1 August 1916. North Sheen station has not yet been built and the London and South Western Railway has withdrawn its service from Richmond to Waterloo and Ludgate Hill via Kew Gardens which it did in 1916. (Mayfair Cards of London, 081-570-7458)

Richmond Green, *c.* 1905, showing the Theatre of 1899. The Green attracted the middle classes because it was close to an old royal centre, the Palace. A similar pattern can be seen at Kew where the Green was formed around the entrance to Kew Gardens and at Ham where the Green leads to the entrance to Ham House.

Richmond Little Green and Presbyterian Church, *c.* 1915, was built 1884–5 and designed by W. Wallace. It opened in May 1885 with seats for 500. Nearby is Richmond Public Library opened in 1881, the first in London.

Richmond Postmen, *c.* 1907, on The Green, Richmond. The main post office on George Street was built in 1886 and is now an HMV store. The growth in houses meant an increased work force was needed to cope with the increased workload.

RICHMOND. — *The Parish Church.*

St Mary Magdalene, Church Walk, *c.* 1906, is the old parish church between green and hill, the oldest part of Richmond nearest to Richmond Palace, with a tower built in 1507.

The Free Church, Ormond Road, Richmond, *c.* 1912, was built in 1912 for the Unitarians with five stained glass lancets by Morris & Co. It was one of many Nonconformist Christian denominations (Unitarian, Congregational and Roman Catholic) who built churches around the Vineyard on the eastern side of Richmond Hill.

St Elizabeth's Roman Catholic Church, The Vineyard, *c.* 1910, built in 1824. The Chancel and tower were rebuilt in 1903. The Congregational Church was built next door five years later in 1831.

Ellerker College, Richmond, *c.* 1910, was Gothicised with stucco walls and turrets in 1808 by Mrs Ellerker. It is similar in design to Gothicised buildings in Ewell, Surrey designed by H. Kitchen in 1810. The Gothic House on Petersham Road, now demolished, was the only other example of this design in Richmond.

The schoolroom of Richmond Hill School or Ellerker College. It had been a school since the 1880s, formerly Ellerker House where the Houblons lived who founded the Houblon Almshouses in Sheen Road. It became the Old Vicarage School in 1931.

St Matthias, Church Road, Richmond, 1911, was designed by Sir Gilbert Scott in 1858 with a spire of 195 feet. It was completed in 1861–2 and a choir vestry added in 1884. The tallest church is the Church of England one with Nonconformist churches grouped at the bottom of the hill.

Richmond from the air, 1919, showing St Matthias and the villas on Church Road and the eastern slopes of Richmond Hill.

Church Road, Richmond, c. 1911, with middle class villas on the eastern slopes of the hill. Chancellors was an old established firm adjoining the station and was active in selling houses in the 1890s. Albert Chancellor was Mayor of Richmond 1902–03.

The Terrace, Richmond Hill, *c.* 1905, and the hut for the superintendent of the Terrace Gardens.

Richmond Hill, 1909, showing the houses at the top of the hill with a view over the river and near to Richmond Park. A policeman is standing on the pavement as carts pass by.

Richmond Terrace, 1909, and nannies sitting with their charges (children) in bassonets (prams). The children were probably the sons and daughters of the owners of the houses behind.

RICHMOND TERRACE   2309

Richmond Terrace, c. 1910, in front of a four-storey terrace of houses. It is probably a colder day as there are no nannies with bassonets on the benches and the woman approaching has a muffler.

The Wesleyan College, Queens Road, Richmond, *c.* 1900, was built as the Wesleyan Theological Institution and opened in 1843 on Friars Stile Road in grounds of 13 acres.

The Lecture Room of the Wesleyan College, *c.* 1908. The dining hall of the College contains a number of Wesley relics including the actual pulpit from the Foundry Chapel, Moorfields, occupied by the founder of Methodism, John Wesley.

Richmond College (the Wesleyan College) with a group photograph of lecturers and students in 1912. It was a training college for ministers and missionaries and formed one of the schools of the University of London.

Representation of a Brahmin wedding at Richmond College, c. 1907. The Brahmin were the highest caste in the Hindu religion.

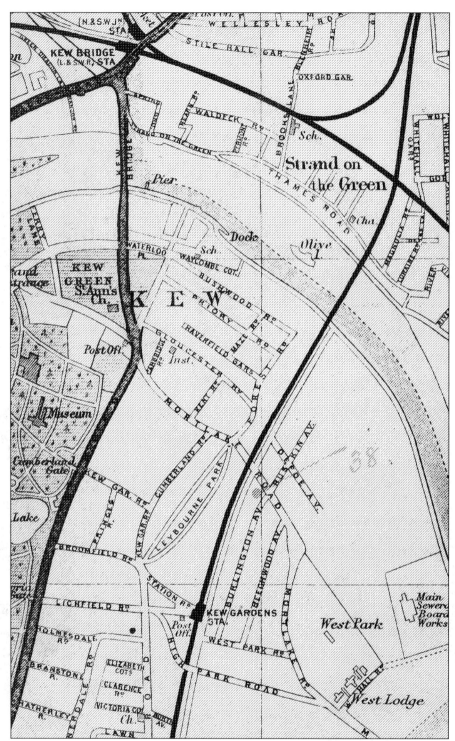

A map of Kew Gardens *c.* 1905 before the building of the thirties Popham estate. The Engleheart (1890–2), Selwyn (1888–92), Priory (1890–2), Leybourne-Popham (1902–06), and the West Park (1902–06) estates have all been built.

Kew Gardens Station and Station Parade, *c. 1909*. The station was built by the London and South Western Railway 1869–9 in yellow brick and was similar to Gunnersbury Station. The shop on the corner belongs to a butcher, Banks & Co., and is now Victor Lown, an estate agent.

Kew Gardens Station and Station Parade, *c. 1909*, from Lichfield Road. It includes the confectioner's shop of H. Lotz who also had two other shops in Richmond at Friars Stile Road and Hill Street. The shop of H. Lotz is now The Kew Greenhouse cafe. The name of the London and South Western Railway is on the front of the station.

The main entrance of Kew Gardens, *c.* 1905, attracted the middle classes to build around the Green making it an exclusive place to live even today.

St Anne's Church, Kew on the Green, *c.* 1905, was built 1710–14 as a chapel. It was lengthened in 1768 and about 1885 the polygonal clock turret was added at the west end. The east end was rebuilt with a lead-covered half dome for the mausoleum for the Duke and Duchess of Cambridge, 1850–1. North vestries were added in 1902.

Kew Parade on the Green, 1910, with the King's Head rebuilt in a mock-Tudor style which became popular in the twenties and thirties.

Waterloo Place, *c.* 1910, on Kew Green, built in 1816, was probably named after the battle. The horse-drawn delivery carts include a brewer's dray with a barrel outside The Greyhound and a cart advertising Liptons Tea and with an address of Cadby Hall, Kensington. The sign on the tree has a notice about football and hockey.

Gloucester House School schoolroom, c. 1905, with gas lights. The school was converted from Gloucester House built in 1750 on the Engleheart estate.

Gloucester House School dining room, c. 1905. It was a major house on the Engleheart estate not owned by the Englehearts as it was bought by a Jewish family, the Neumagens, who ran it as a private girls' school from 1840 to 1919 and benefited from the conversion of the market gardens to middle class housing estates

Gloucester House School croquet lawn, *c.* 1905, with mallets and hoops. Other sports played included netball.

The Nut Walk in the grounds of Gloucester House School, *c.*1905, with some girls reading. It shows the space and countryside in the grounds before houses surrounded the school. The House was demolished in 1928 and Gloucester Court was built on the site.

Kew Road, *c.* 1910, with the tram line in the middle of the road. When Kew Gardens Station was built the landowners began to realise the potential value of their estates and a long succession of auctions (1892–1911) saw the large properties split up and new streets laid. The estates included the Engleheart (1890–2), Selwyn (1888–92), Priory (1890–2), Leybourne-Popham (1902–06) and the West Park (1902–06) estates.

Kew Gardens Road, *c.* 1910, was part of the Engleheart estate (1892–94) which included Gloucester Road, part of Mortlake Road and Cumberland Road. It extended Sandycombe Lane from its old route along Broomfield Road.

Leybourne Park, c. 1905, backing on to the railway was part of the Leybourne-Popham estate. The development of 1902 also included Our Lady of Loreto and St Winefride's Roman Catholic Church built in 1906 on Leybourne Park.

West Park Road, c. 1910, was built from 1902 on the estates of John Poupart and James Pocock. The development included West Park Road, Burlington, Beechwood, Ruskin and Defoe Avenues and a row of shops called West Park Exchange.

This view of Kew from the air, although a later picture, *c.* 1919, shows the spread of the Selwyn estate which stretched from Selwyn Avenue to Lichfield Road, named after George Selwyn, Bishop of Lichfield.

Lawn Crescent was part of the Selwyn estate and was soon patronised by visiting tradesmen, in this case by the carts of the local dairy, probably Hornby's, advertising pure milk and serving St Margarets, Richmond and Kew.

St Luke's Vicarage, c. 1905, next to St Luke's church on The Avenue. A plot was made available on Sandycombe Lane but it was too small and St Luke's was built on The Avenue. St Luke's Church of England School was built on the site instead.

St Luke's, The Avenue, Kew Gardens built in 1888 when the development of the Selwyn estate expanded the parish of St Anne's so much that a new parish of St Luke's was created complete with church, 1892–1911. It was converted and extended as a day centre in 1980.

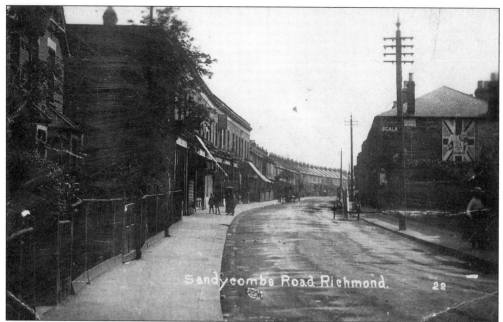

Sandycombe Road, Richmond, *c.* 1905, with a row of shops and a crescent of terraced houses on the left and on the right a patriotic wall painting of a bulldog against a Union Jack. It also included the Victoria Parade row of shops.

Sandycombe Road, Kew, *c.* 1906, outside the row of terraced houses. It was once known as Sandy Lane and ran parallel with North Road and the railway to Kew Gardens. It was along the railway that the smaller houses were built.

North Road, 1901, with a London and South Western Railway train approaching. The complex of houses around Darell Road, Dancer Road and Chilton Road have already been built. Morris & Sons bakery is now Lance Owen, a car dealership. Under the bridge there was a siding for the gas works.

Lower Mortlake Road, Richmond, c. 1906, before the right side was rebuilt and widened in the thirties. The shop on the corner of Salisbury Road was Freeman & Co. a boot and shoe manufacturer. The milk cart is from the Walia Dairy of Tom Thomas.

ST JOHN'S CHURCH RICHMOND

St John the Divine, Kew Road, *c.* 1913, next to the railway station, was built 1831–6 and designed by Lewis Vulliamy who also designed Hickey's Almshouses 1832–5. It was a Commissioners church and served the area known as Lower Richmond along Kew Road and the smaller houses along the railway line and Lower Mortlake Road.

Holy Trinity, Townshend Road, Richmond, c. 1905, opened at the same time as the parish in 1870 at a cost of £10,000 including a £1,000 organ. The tower was added in 1880 but was demolished about 1970 and a porch has recently been added.

Sheen Road, Richmond, c. 1910, with its parade of shops was a bus route for the General's no. 37 going to Herne Hill. The shops with the blinds up include Bowman & Co., a grocers, and Rudman & Co., a family butcher.

Hickey's Almshouses Gates, Sheen Road, with two General route no. 37s passing. Route 37 ran between Hounslow Heath and Peckham via Sheen Road. The nearer bus is going to Herne Hill via Upper Richmond Road and the one approaching is going to Hounslow via Richmond. (Lens of Sutton)

Hickey's Almshouses gates, *c.* 1910, Sheen Road, Richmond built 1832–35 by Lewis Vulliamy, who also designed St John the Divine (1831–6).

Queens Road, Richmond, *c.* 1900, with a name reflecting Richmond's royal past. The tower at the end of the road belongs to Trinity Church.

The Marist Convent, Queens Road, Richmond, c.1915, a Roman Catholic boarding and day school for girls, opened based on the Jesuit Rule.

The entrance hall of the Marist Convent, c. 1915, with religious pictures and statues. The Marists (Society of Mary) did parish work, taught in schools and seminaries, and held home missions and chaplaincies.

Marist Convent, Richmond.

The girls playing tennis on grass at the Marist Convent, *c.* 1915. The order was founded in 1816 by Jean Claude Courveille and Jean Claude Marie Colin, the order held that Mary desired to aid the church through a namesake congregation. There was also a Marist convent for girls at Parsons Green opened in 1895.

Marist Convent, Richmond.

The courtyard of the Marist Convent, *c.* 1915. It was damaged during the war and plans were made for a Catholic Secondary School, St Edward the Confessor R.C. Secondary School. Today the site is occupied by Christ's School West Side.

A patriotic scene outside St Andrews National School, Ham Street, Ham, on Coronation Day 1911 . The school was bought by local charities, public subscription and the National Society in 1877 to avoid having 'to endure the extravagances of the Board School system'. In 1966 the school was sold and converted into St Thomas Aquinas Roman Catholic Church.

The Library, Petersham Road was Farm Lodge, a gate lodge for the Petersham Lodge estate. The room looking on to the road was used as a reading room for the Petersham branch of Richmond Free Library 1900–08 which was closed due to lack of use.

The Twickenham Ferry, *c.* 1903, operating between Twickenham and Ham gave access to the Petersham Rifle Club as well as Ham House. The view here shows the Twickenham bank.

Richmond Royal Hospital, Kew Foot Road, *c.* 1915, was bought in 1868 as Rosedale House from the Earl of Shaftesbury and was opened as the Richmond Infirmary By Earl Russell. The Duchess of Teck (Princess Mary Adelaide) who lived at the White Lodge, Richmond Park, opened new wards in 1882. In 1897 Queen Victoria gave permission for it to be called the Royal Hospital. It overlooked the Royal Richmond Horseshow ground.

Terrace Gardens entrance, *c.* 1915. They were originally attached to Buccleuch House. It was bought by the Richmond Vestry in 1886 for £30,000 who sold the House and kept the gardens. The Town Council bought the House itself in 1938 and demolished it to make a garden and continue the tow-path.

The Terrace Gardens greenhouse, *c.* 1915, was part of the landscaping which was opened to the public on 21 May 1887 by the Duchess of Teck.

The Terrace Gardens Ornamental Fountain, c. 1915, was the site of a mansion owned by the Marquis of Lansdowne, the foundations of which still remain. It was then bought by the Duke of Buccleuch.

In 1891 the newly-formed Richmond Corporation of 1890 built a memorial outside the Gates of Richmond Park to commemorate the interest of the Duchess of Teck in Richmond, especially the Royal Hospital. The Morshesad (Richmond Gate) Hotel is shown behind.

Town Hall,
Richmond.

The Town Hall, Hill Street, Richmond, *c.* 1910, cost £24,000 and was opened on 10 June 1893 by the future King George V (then the Duke of York). The site of the Town Hall, including the old Castle Hotel, was bought in 1888 by Sir Whittaker-Ellis who presented the ground for the Town Hall, the road at the side and the garden to the Corporation.

New Bridge and Lock, Richmond-on-Thames

The new Footbridge and Lock, unique on the Thames, was built at a cost of £60,000 and was opened by King George V and Queen Mary (then Duke and Duchess of York) on 19 May 1894. It was built with three sluices, each 66 feet wide, which could be lowered to control the flow of water when the river was in flood. A large lock on the Surrey side allows heavy traffic to pass when the sluices are down.

Richmond County School for boys, Kew Road, *c.* 1905, opened in 1895, became a Technical Institute in 1939 and then an Institute for Higher Education and has now been converted for housing.

Socialites at Richmond Royal Horse Show, *c.* 1910, showing Edwardian fashions for men and women during the three days in June when it was held. It was regarded nationally as the principal horse show and was held annually until 1967.

Richmond Royal Horse Show with a parade of traps, c. 1905. It was founded by a syndicate of gentlemen in 1892. The first president was the Duke of Teck who was usually accompanied by the Duchess.

Richmond Royal Horse Show with a parade of carriages, c. 1905. King Edward VII and Queen Alexandra (as Prince and Princess of Wales) and King George V and Queen Mary (1913) attended up to the outbreak of the First World War.

Kew Bridge before and after rebuilding, 1899–1903. It was designed by Sir John Wolfe Barry and Cuthbert Bereton and opened by King Edward VII on 20 May 1903.

Kew Bridge, c. 1909, looking to the Chiswick side with a tug just passing underneath the middle of the three elliptical arches in grey granite.

The new Richmond Theatre Royal and Opera House, *c.* 1905, on the Little Green was designed by Frank Matcham and opened to the public on Monday 18 September 1899. Ben Greet and his company presented *As You Like It* for the opening week.

The Secondary School for girls, Parkshot, Richmond, *c.* 1908, was built in 1908. Richmond Council also built Darell Road School (1906) and Gainsborough Road Secondary School (1912–13) in Kew. The Richmond Secondary School closed in 1974 and became Richmond Adult Education College.

George Street, Richmond, c. 1906, and Gosling and Sons the drapers, established 1795. Opposite is a T. Foster & Co. cart in front of its wine merchants' shop. The tower of the electricity station is in the distance. George III gave his name to the main street in Richmond, like Croydon.

George Street, Richmond, c. 1906. Wright Bros Ltd are on the left and on the right with the blinds up are Lilley and Skinner Ltd, boot and shoe manufacturers, and Lipton. Outside W. Cornell, a carrier and contractor is delivering and a horse-drawn bus is going down George Street towards the river.

George Street, Richmond, c. 1910. On the left is a bank, H.B. Boggs shoe shop, and Boots the chemist, who had this card produced. A General bus on route no. 37 is coming down George Street, as is a policeman on the right of the picture.

Bridge Street, Richmond, c. 1910, with a B-type motor bus on General route no. 37 to Hounslow having passed another no. 37 to Herne Hill and with a no. 27 behind. At the back of all the buses is the building which preceded the Odeon, and on the left with the Italian villa tower is Tower House.

George Street, Richmond, *c*.1917. A.W. Poppy's ladies' wear shop on the left is next to Fuller's chocolate shop and behind that there is a sign reading Post Office Public Telephone. Opposite is Reynolds & Co.'s ironmongers shop.

King Street, Richmond, *c*. 1910, preserves the royal connection. On the left is Joseph Mears' shop offering steam launches for hire; S. Abell & Co., a goldsmith; and W. Rickett, a plumber, gas and hot water fitter. Shops on the right include a motor cycle works and King Street Dining Rooms. The sign points to London.

Hill Street, Richmond, *c.* 1914, looking back to the Queen's Head Hotel. On the left on the corner of Whittaker Avenue is Ellis & Co. with the Heron Corner house behind. On the right is the van of T.W. Breach, a cash draper, and behind that is the Victoria servants registry, a high class servant agency. I.T. Herrington and Son with the coat of arms is a ticket agent for the theatre and railway companies.

Hill Rise, Richmond, *c.* 1914. On the left is the Rose Cottage tea rooms and on the right Lascelles, Tickner & Co. offering ales and cider, and San Toy, a confectioner selling Cadburys chocolates as well as pots of tea, cream ices, ices, soda, and milk.

A CHILD STUDY

W. S. Stuart,
Court Photographer
2 The Quadrant,
Richmond, Surrey
TELEPHONE - 248 P.O. RICHMOND

BY APPOINTMENT

W.S. Stuart Royal Appointments, 2 The Quadrant, Richmond, *c.* 1910. Any association by the middle class shop owners with royalty was good for business as shown by Herrington and Sons in Richmond and Newens the bakers at Kew.

The Quadrant, Richmond, *c.* 1905, was really the beginning of Kew Road but took its grander title in the 1890s. The picture is taken near the London & South Western Railway station with the South Western Hotel on the left which is Drummonds wine bar today.

The Quadrant, Richmond, *c.* 1911, bedecked with Union Jacks and a taxi rank in the middle of the road. A sign on the left advertises the Shepherd's Bush Empire and adds to the patriotic feeling of the picture.

Robin Hood Gate Richmond Park

The Robin Hood Gate, Richmond Park, c. 1905, is on the boundary of the Borough of Richmond. Richmond Park was one of the attractions opened up for day trippers by the motor bus.

Richmond Park, c. 1905, with a party of Edwardian women, children and a dog going for a walk. The Park has an area of 2,538 acres and a circumference of 10 miles.

Pen Ponds, *c.* 1914, near White Lodge, Richmond Park, were stocked with fish but could only be used by anglers with special permission. It was an area where water rose through the London Clay.

Deer in Richmond Park, *c.* 1914. Both Fallow and red deer are kept in the Park, a reminder of the days when King Charles I and the nobility hunted in it as a royal park. However, by the Edwardian era they were enjoyed as part of nature.

The Terrace, Richmond, c. 1914, with a crowd of people promenading, probably a Bank Holiday crowd brought by motor bus. The Mansion Hotel, which is now the Petersham Hotel, is behind.

Boat maintenance outside the Castle Assembly Rooms, Richmond, c. 1905. The row boats in the river are ready for visitors and behind them are barges. The building is the White Cross Hotel and behind that is the railway bridge.

Punts and row boats for hire probably on a weekend or Bank Holiday *c.* 1912 at Richmond on the Ham side of the bridge. This was another attraction for the visitors who had come by motor bus. A tug is going up stream towards Messums boatyard.

The backwater from Richmond Bridge, *c.* 1912, shows Maynards, a boat and yacht builder at the back of Corporation Island. Other builders included J. Glover on Glover's Island at Petersham and Messums Boatyard at Richmond.

The Original shop for Maids of Honour, Hill Street, *c.* 1905, 'established in Richmond nearly 200 years'. The name for the cheese tartlet comes from the maids of honour of Caroline of Anspach, Princess of Wales, who lived at the Maids of Honour Row on the Green, built in 1724.

Hill Street, Richmond, c. 1914. On the left are W. Herbert Yates, a picture framer, the Cosy Corner Tea rooms with a balcony overlooking river, the empty motor garage of Hurst Park & Co., and The Globe Tea Rooms.

The Orchestra Lounge, Hill Cottage Tea Rooms, 54/56 Hill Rise, Richmond. It advertised itself as 'The famous Tea Rooms, near River Terrace and Park. Patronised by travellers from all parts of the world'.

The Star and Garter Hotel, Richmond, *c.* 1914, was designed by E.M. Barry in the 'French Chateau' style in 1865. It closed in 1907 and was used as a hospital for soldiers during the First World War. It was then demolished and the Star and Garter Home was built on top of it.

The Star and Garter Hotel exterior of annexe, *c.* 1914. The annexe was also known as the banqueting suite and was built in 1874 to replace an earlier pavilion which burnt down.

Richmond Hill Hotel, Richmond Hill, *c.* 1913. It was originally Mansfield House built *c.* 1720. The two wings were added 1841–3, it became the Queen's Hotel in 1875 and changed its name to the Richmond Hill Hotel in 1913.

Metcalfe's Hydro, Richmond Hill, Surrey, *c.* 1910. The name suggests that it was probably a health centre using water in the therapy.

Horse-drawn trams on Kew Green outside the Coach and Horses, *c.* 1907. There was a tramway to Shepherds Bush on the other side of the bridge but no tram link so passengers had to walk over it themselves to continue their journey. There was no depot to service the trams on the Kew side so they had to be taken over the bridge to be overhauled.

Trams operated by London United Tramways ran from the Orange Tree, Kew Road, to Kew Bridge from 1883 to 1912 and the last one on the last day of operation is shown here. The shed is now an Arts centre.

Mortlake Terrace, Kew, *c.* 1910 with a motor bus at the junction of the Mortlake Road and Kew Road. The shops on the right include Mills and Winsall, a grocer and Edwards, a chemist. During road widening in the thirties the buildings on the left hand corner were demolished.

The Coach and Horses, Kew Green, *c.* 1910 with a General route no. 27 which ran between Hounslow and Highgate. The Richmond Vestry blocked plans for an electric tramway linking the trams either side of the river. In response London United withdrew the tram service (1912) and a replacement bus route no. 27 was introduced instead.

The Victoria Gates, Kew Gardens, *c.* 1900, with a North London Railway poster was the most convenient for visitors arriving at Kew Gardens Station.

In addition to the Palm and Temperate Houses there were the lesser known T-range houses numbered 7 to 14 and named after their shape. They were replaced by the Princess of Wales Conservatory opened in 1987. No. 4 Greenhouse, shown here *c.* 1910, was the original conservatory devoted to the display of flowers in season.

The Palmhouse, Kew Gardens, *c.* 1912, was designed by Decimus Burton and built 1844–48 for palms and tropical plants with five miles of hot water pipes. It was finished three years before the even larger greenhouse of Joseph Paxton at Hyde Park for the Great Exhibition of 1851.

The Temperate House, Kew Gardens, *c.* 1912, was the second greenhouse designed by Decimus Burton and built between 1860 and 1898. It was designed for the cultivation of plants unable to tolerate the British winter.

The Pagoda, *c.* 1907, was designed by Sir William Chambers with 10 octagonal storeys and was built 1761–2. It had more decorations when first built as each corner of each roof had a multicoloured varnished dragon with a bell in its mouth.

The Tea Rooms, Kew Gardens, *c.* 1910, were burnt down during February 1913 by two Suffragettes because the Gardens were perceived to be a famous establishment social centre. They were replaced in 1915 during the First World War.

The Tea Rooms on Kew Green, *c.* 1911, were perfectly placed for visitors travelling on London United Tramway's trams to Kew Bridge and crossing over to Kew Gardens.

Kew Gardens Hotel, Sandycombe Road, Kew, c. 1910, is a reflection of the number of visitors to the Gardens since there were enough visitors to support a hotel in Kew. The Lonsdale confectioners shop selling Fry's chocolate is now a launderette.

The 'Olde English Fayre', Kew Green, on the 22 July 1914, the summer before the outbreak of the First World War on 5 August 1914.

Two

First World War

Richmond Park Camp, c. 1914, in the Roehampton Paddocks west of Sheen cross roads was occupied by the London Scottish Regiment during May 1915. It was probably a territorial unit attached to the 51st (London) Division and its name may be preserved in Richmond by the London Scottish rugby club.

The entrance to the South African War Hospital, Richmond Park, *c*. 1915. A second pedestrian gate, Cambrian Road Gate, was provided specifically to serve this unit.

The huts of the South African War Hospital, Richmond Park, *c*. 1915, were built on the parkland between Conduit Wood and Bishop's Lodge. South African forces made up 11 per cent of the white male Dominion forces serving overseas in the armed forces.

The South African War Hospital, Richmond Park, with a water tower behind the huts. It later became the Ministry of Pensions Hospital and was the last of the camps to survive until demolition in 1925.

The Red Cross Hospital, Richmond Green, c. 1914. The Star and Garter Hotel was also a Red Cross Hospital and the Royal Hospital was one of the first hospitals out of London to accommodate wounded soldiers from the Front. Soldiers were also looked after at the nearby Grove Road Hospital.

A fancy dress football match given by the employees of the Whitehead Aircraft Co. Ltd., in Old
Deer Park, Richmond, 11 December 1915, in aid of the Red Cross Fund.

A presentation to the Works Manager on completion of the Whitehead Aircraft Co. extension.
The factory had been bought by the Company in 1915 to make planes. The first building was a
Drill Hall on Townshend Terrace but this was extended to Grena Road and Manor Park. The
company collapsed in 1922 probably because the end of war production had slowed the orders
and the company was sold.

Three
Twenties and Thirties

General Smuts in Richmond Cemetery, Grove Road, on 1 July 1921 unveiling a memorial to the South African soldiers who died in the South African Hospital in Richmond Park during the Great War with the Bishop of St Albans and the Mayor and Alderman Sir James Slumper in attendance. The memorial was an obelisk carved with a springbok.

Richmond War Memorial outside the Town Hall by the river was built by the people of Richmond and unveiled on 23 November 1921 by Field Marshal Sir William Robertson-Bart.

The Star and Garter Home for disabled sailors and soldiers, *c.* 1926, was designed free of charge by Sir Edwin Cooper and was built from a fund raised by the women of the Empire. It was built 1921–4 by Messrs Mowlem & Co. in a Neo-Georgian style in red brick and Portland Stone.

The Star and Garter 1924. 'Imposing with its tall columns and its stone parapet, it has dormer windows and red tiled roofs, giving it the appearance of a real home for those broken in our wars' (Arthur Mee, 1955). It included rooms for 186, workshops, a common room and a cinema theatre.

An aerial view, *c.* 1925, of Richmond Hill showing the Star and Garter Home and looking down Queens Road. The Home, once a hotel itself, is still surrounded by them with The Mansion Hotel (renamed the new Star and Garter 1924) on the left and the Richmond Hill Hotel and the Morshead (Richmond Gate Hotel) in front.

The Q Laundry van, *c.* 1925, which may have serviced the numerous hotels on Richmond Hill. It sits outside Warwick Motors who probably finished the body of the van. Today the site of the laundry has been replaced by offices.

The Hotel Stuart, Richmond Hill, *c*. 1920, is the building on the left with the clock in front of it. It is amongst the group of hotels at the top of Richmond Hill overlooking The Terrace.

The Morshead Hotel, Richmond Hill, *c*. 1925, now the Richmond Gate Hotel, was one of the hotels that replaced the lost business of the Star and Garter Hotel.

George Street, Richmond, *c.* 1924, with two open top buses of the General Company outside Goslings with the leading bus on route 73 to Stoke Newington. On the right the blinds are down on Slaters and M.W. Yallop.

GEORGE ST RICHMOND

4366

George Street, Richmond, *c.* 1924. A horse-drawn delivery van is outside Goslings and a bus is coming towards the camera. Goslings was opened in 1795 and expanded into the Queen's Head. After a fire in 1968 it closed down and re-opened as Dickens and Jones in 1970.

Hill Street and a K type bus on General route no. 65A which ran from Ealing to Hook via Ealing Broadway, Brentford High Street, Kew Road, Richmond Road, Kingston and Surbiton. Buses now extended well beyond Richmond. (Lens of Sutton)

Petersham Road and Hill Rise, *c*. 1924, showing how narrow the road was before it was widened *c*. 1935 and the houses were demolished. An open top bus on General route 73 to Petersham waits for another 73 to come through.

The Terrace, Richmond, *c.* 1921 was still as popular with visitors in the twenties as it had been in the Edwardian era.

Richmond Park, *c.* 1919. The main difference with the Edwardian visitor was that now people could drive through it in cars as well as walk.

The river at Richmond, *c.* 1924, with a Thames steamer heading towards Teddington Lock. The Star and Garter Home has replaced the Hotel and the new Star and Garter Hotel is on the left.

RIVER AT RICHMOND   2601

Messums and Pigeon's Hotel, August 1924. The business was developed from a single boat-house, a small beer house and sheds by Richard Henry Messum, a King's Waterman who died on 15 December 1914. Messrs. Messum were famous for their skiffs and built for nearly all the crown heads of Europe.

Richmond from the bridge, *c.* 1931. On the far left is the Castle Restaurant and Ball Room and on the far right Tower House has become Nuthalls Restaurant. Underneath were four lock ups occupied by H. & A. Rednap, punt, boat and dinghy builders and J. Peaslake and Son.

Richmond from the river with visitors promenading, *c.* 1931. The Union Jack is flying and a boat is being mended on the bank while most of the boats appear to have been hired. The 1933 road bridge is yet to be built and the White Cross Hotel is behind the crowds.

The riverside for boating at Richmond, c. 1931. A crowd watch while people are hiring a rowing boat in front of the bridge, which was widened in 1937.

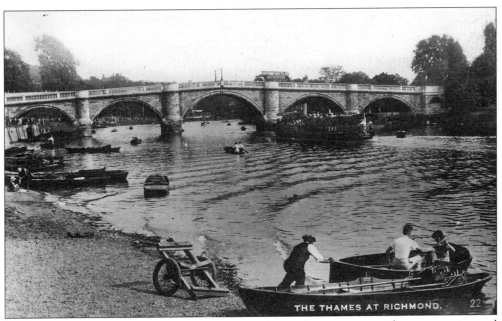

THE THAMES AT RICHMOND. 22

The Thames at Richmond, c. 1931, showing two forms of amusement on the river, rowing and pleasure cruising. A General bus is crossing over the bridge at the same time as a Thames pleasure cruiser is going under it.

A Thames Pleasure Steamer, *c.* 1927, with the life jackets lining the sides and cabins underneath. These types of boat operated between Richmond and the piers in London.

A group of men and women on a Thames Pleasure Steamer at Richmond, *c.* 1925. The life-jackets line the rails and behind some of the group must be standing on the benches. A lone man looks on from the bank and behind him are rugby posts perhaps in the Old Deer Park.

The landing stage at Richmond on a busy weekend, c. 1931. The houses backing onto the river had their fronts on Petersham Road.

The Lock at Teddington, c. 1931 is on the boundaries of the Borough of Richmond. A Thames cruiser has just passed through and there is a steam crane on the left.

Kew Gardens by District Railway Direct 1923 by Irene Fawkes. At this time the District Railway had been part of the Underground since 1908 (London Transport Museum).

An aerial view of Kew Gardens, c. 1920, which shows the layout of the Gardens around the Palm House. On the right are the houses of the Priory and Engleheart estates in Kew. On the opposite bank is the tower of the waterworks.

Kew Gardens, c. 1920, with a man and two women outside the greenhouses near Kew Road. The twenties women's fashions of bonnet hats, furs, long pearl necklaces and shoes with single straps are well modelled here.

KEW GARDENS *from the Air*

Kew Gardens from the air, c. 1920. The Temperate House, the Pagoda and Palm House are in this view. The 225 foot Douglas fir flagpole from Vancouver is harder to find between the Temperate House and Kew Road.

Flora House on Kew Green, c. 1922. Will Evans came to Kew in 1913 and opened a string of tea shops including Flora House on Kew Green to catch the passing trade of visitors to the Gardens.

The Will Evans Restaurant or The Imperial Restaurant and The Dieudonne on Kew Green, c. 1920, were both owned by Will Evans. The Dieudonne had been built in 1919 after the previous building, Snailwell House, had been damaged by fire.

The back garden of The Will Evans Restaurant on Kew Green, c. 1920. The tables are decorated with chequered tea cloths and umbrellas and the seating includes deck chairs. Tea Gardens were very popular in Surrey towns in the twenties.

Bluebell Time in Kew Gardens and the General Country 1931 by Margaret Calkin James with a pattern recognisable in black and white. The London Passenger Transport Board (London Transport) was not formed until 1933 when General merged with the Underground Group. (London Transport Museum)

An NS type bus with a covered top on General route no 37L in the London suburbs, c. 1925. Route 37L went via the Upper Richmond Road, High Street Wandsworth, and the Old Kent Road to Peckham on a west-east route.

General route no 33A, weekday only, near Hyde Park Corner on its way to Richmond in the days when buses from Richmond went to the West End. The headboard reads Waterloo Bridge, Strand, Charing +, Piccadily, Hyde Park Corner, Knightsbridge, Albert Hall, Kensington Church, Hammersmith Bway, Castelnau, Upper Richmond Road, RICHMOND. (Lens of Sutton)

Manor Farm Dairy, Ham Street, Ham, c. 1927. Dairy farming in Richmond was mainly on the rich floodplains by the river where there was good pasture land.

Long and Pocock's or Clifford's Dairy, serving East Sheen but on 424 Upper Richmond Road at the junction with Cliffords Avenue. Long and Pocock also had another dairy at Northfields on the other side of the river. The main offices are now occupied by Caesarstone The Granite and Marble Specialists and the building with the chimney is Sheens Hand Carwash.

THE MODEL DAIRIES AND

CREAMERIES,

12 The Quadrant, RICHMOND, ...

16 Station Parade. KEW GARDENS, .

AND

The Broadway, ST. MARGARET'S, S.W.

F. & H. E. HORNBY.

Hornby's advert of 1899. Hornby were the other main dairy in Richmond.

The Ministry of Labour Claims and Records Offices off Ruskin Avenue, Kew, in 1929 were built after the war on land to the east of the railway.

The front entrance of the Record Offices, Kew, 1925. During the sixties the site was redeveloped with the Crown Building (1967–9) and the Public Record Office (1973–77). At the time of writing an extension to the Public Records Office is being built (1994–5), while the Crown building on stilts overlooking the Thames lies derelict.

The Occupation Road, 1928, showing how trees were cleared to avoid the problem of falling leaves causing slipping on the tracks. The car is on the edge of the flooded area and a plank bridge has been built to give access to the offices.

A view of the flooding from the railway embankment on 7 January 1928. The Records Office was nearest the River Thames so the water was at its highest here.

The main gates of the Records Office 1928 with flooding up to the ankles. A group of people are huddled under the porch of the front entrance. This picture can be compared with the view of the front entrance when it was dry.

The main gates from the Records Office looking down the partially flooded Defoe Avenue, Kew, 1928. A milk cart appears to be making its rounds as far as possible.

Defoe Avenue, Kew, looking towards the main gates of the Records Office with a group of residents awaiting instructions on 7 January 1928. It looks as if this picture was taken from a top floor window which was probably a safe place to be.

A rowing boat on Kew Green looking towards Waterloo Place during the flooding in 1928 in which 500 homes were flooded in Kew.

Richmond Hill Court, Richmond Hill, 1928. Other flats built in Richmond in the twenties and thirties include Gloucester Court (1928) and Lichfield Court (1933) designed by Bertram Carter.

RICHMOND HILL COURT.

Richmond Hill Court, Richmond Hill, 1928. It was finished in red brick and was designed around a crescent with tennis courts in the middle.

The Dysart Arms, Petersham, c. 1922, rebuilt in mock-Tudor in 1902 outside the gates of a Tudor Park. The Dysarts lived at Ham House and held manorial rights. The Dysart Arms also ran a garage and a 1921 telephone box is outside.

The Ranelagh Harriers, 1930–31, were an athletic club who moved to the Dysart Arms, Petersham. The twenties and thirties saw people with more leisure time for sports.

Richmond Station in 1932, before rebuilding. At Richmond there were in effect two stations; the platforms for Waterloo trains crossed about midway by the overbridge carrying Kew Road, and on the north and east of Kew Road five terminal bays used by the Underground District line and London Midland and Scottish electric trains. Each railway company had its own offices. (London Transport Museum)

North Sheen

North Sheen, a strip of land stretching from Kew Railway Bridge to Richmond Park, was attached to Mortlake until 1892, when the new Richmond Borough incorporated it. The area already included Kew Gardens Station and Richmond Gas works. Manor Grove estate was built around the Gas Works by the Richmond Corporation in 1894 under the Workmen's Dwellings Act. Further houses were built near the Gas Works around Darell Road including a school (1905) and further north houses were built around Kew Gardens Station at the West Park estate including the West Park Exchange row of shops.

The area in between was filled in during the twenties and thirties beginning with West Park Avenue in 1925. In advance of further building a church (1929) and railway station (1930) were built. The Barn Church of St Phillip and All Saints, North Sheen, was originally a sixteenth-century barn of Stonehall Farm at Oxted. When new churches were called for in the diocese the Hoare and Lambert families offered it. In 1928 it was dismantled and each timber numbered before being brought to the site and reassembled. It cost £5000 to build and was dedicated by the Bishop of Southwark during February 1929. It became the centre of the thirties Popham Estate including Pensford, Nylands, Beehive and Taylor Avenues. Pensford Avenue was built in 1936 with some houses for £1500 built in the grounds of Reston House. The Southern Railway provided two concrete footbridges at Kew Gardens Station and another linking North Road and Sandycombe Road for the new residents of the estate.

The Great Chertsey Road cut through the area in 1933 when Lower Mortlake Road and Lower Richmond Road were widened to join the two new bridges linking Twickenham (1928–33) and Chiswick (1933). The remaining space was filled by North Sheen and Hammersmith cemeteries by 1932.

North Sheen Station, opened on 6 July 1930 by the Southern Railway at the same time as the line from Waterloo to Windsor was electrified. It was built for new residential traffic. (Lens of Sutton)

North Sheen Station, 1930, with a 520 feet island platform, a modest canopied shelter, and a small ticket office, was reached by a footpath and footbridge which has been replaced by a new one only recently. The allotments are on the right and the backs of the houses of Manor Grove are on the left. (Lens of Sutton)

The Richmond Railway Bridge was built in 1908 to the design of the engineer J.W. Jacomb Hood with three 100 feet span arches. It is shown here with a Southern Railway electric multiple unit crossing it before the 1933 road bridge carrying the Great Chertsey Road over the Thames was built by the side of it.

Corporation Island and the Railway Bridge, c. 1931, before the building of the new Richmond-Twickenham Bridge 1928–33.

The new Richmond-Twickenham Bridge 1928–33. The Lower Mortlake Road and Lower Richmond Road were widened to link the two new bridges at Chiswick and Twickenham (see *Chiswick* in the Archive Photographs series).

The new Richmond-Twickenham Bridge was built 1928–33 with three main arches of reinforced concrete. It was the first large concrete bridge on the three-pin principle in this country. It was designed by Alfred Dryland who also designed Chiswick Bridge.

The new Art Deco extension of the British Legion Poppy Factory in Petersham Road, Richmond, was opened in 1933 by H.R.H. Princess Mary, The Princess Royal.

Assembling the poppies in the new Poppy Factory, 1933. The first factory, Watney's Brewery, had been bought in 1925 after the Poppy Factory moved from the Old Kent Road and the first poppies were produced in 1926. Watneys then moved to Mortlake.

Veining the poppies in the Poppy Factory, 1933. The new extension was built after a fire at the factory warehouse at King's Cross. The need for a new warehouse and problems with heating the brewery building at Richmond meant a new structure was needed and the brewery was retained for storage.

Assembling the poppies in the Poppy Factory, 1933. The Museum of Richmond's exhibition 'The Factory of Remembrance: The Poppy and The Royal British Legion Poppy Factory' recently opened, running from November 1994 to February 1995.

Wreath making in the Poppy Factory, 1933. Major George Howson, who was disabled in the war, set up the Disabled Society which put forward the idea that the men could make things and they began by making flowers. He died in 1936.

Rosettes and badges being made at the Poppy Factory, 1933. 'Of the 360 nearly a third are totally disabled, half have lost a leg, and there are almost as many missing limbs as there are men' (Arthur Mee, 1955).

The Poppy Factory extension, 1933, showing its position in the Cardigan House estate which was bought to provide accommodation for the 360 workers at the factory.

Cardigan Flats included the building of 58 flats and a further eight flats converted from other buildings. The first foundation stone for them had been laid in 1926. Lord Cardigan was famous for the Charge of the Light Brigade.

Richmond London Transport Bus Station in 1939 at the back of the shops fronting Red Lion Street just before war broke out. The buses include 1930 LT types with the front canopy on route nos. 37 to Peckham and 73 which ran out along Sheen Road to Stoke Newington via Barnes and Hammersmith. A 1937 STL type on route 73 is just arriving at the bus station while the drivers in white coats are opposite the driver's kiosk. (London Transport Museum).

Richmond London Transport Bus Station with six-wheel LT types lined up by the backs of the shops on Red Lion Street. The leading bus is on route 73 to Stoke Newington via Kensington and Kings Cross. (Lens of Sutton)

Four
Second World War

Air raid trenches being dug on Richmond Green in September 1938 using a cut and cover method of construction. A trench was dug, a wooden frame was inserted and covered by corrugated iron and the tube was then filled over.

Air raid trenches being dug on Richmond Green in September 1938 with a steam excavator helping to dig a trench. Air raid trenches were also built at Kew Green.

A procession of nurses, the St John's Ambulance Brigade, and other civil defence organisations on George Street, Richmond, during April 1941. The streets are packed and the sign for Williamsons Ltd can be seen on the left.

Celebrations for V.E. (Victory in Europe) Day, 9 May 1945, at Waterloo Place off George Street, Richmond. The flags flying include those of the allies, the Union Jack of Britain, the Stars and Stripes of the United States, and the Hammer and Sickle of the Soviet Union.

Richmond and Kew war damage

Richmond and Kew were both near enough to London to suffer bomb damage. Richmond and Kew were near to the factories on the Great West Road and Ham and Petersham were close to the aircraft factory at Kingston. During the Blitz (September 1940 to May 1941), Richmond Town Hall was hit on 29 November 1940. Other hits included the Courtland Flats in Sheen Road, the Marist Convent, the Wesleyan Chapel, the Russell School in Petersham, and Sheen Pond Lodge in Richmond Park. Kew was near to the Great West Road and suffered a recorded 59 bombs. Fortunately, Kew Gardens took more than 30 bombs and many incendiaries doing little damage. However, bomb hits were recorded at Newens Bakery and houses on Kew Road and five raids alone on Beechwood Avenue during 1940. During the V1 campaign (June 1944 to March 1945) one is recorded at Kew and another in 1944 on Trumpeter's House which was used as an American Red Cross Club. The first V2 in London fell on Staveley Road, Chiswick on 8 September 1944 killing three people and badly injuring another 10, the second on 12 September fell on Beechwood Avenue, Kew destroying eight houses. The last two exploded on 27 March 1945 at Bethnal Green killing 133.

Five

Fifties and Sixties

A composite picture showing all the leisure activities in Richmond in 1958 – boating and cruising on the Thames and promenading along the river or in the parks – as well as the no. 27 bus to take you there with a policeman directing traffic over the bridge.

The Quadrant, Richmond, c. 1955, without the traffic lights. On the left is J. Dunn & Co. and Dolcis, and on the right The Fifty Shilling Taylor selling menswear and The Brown Bear pub selling Watneys Ales.

George Street, Richmond, c. 1955, with Wrights Brothers on the left which became Owen and Owen in the sixties until it closed in 1990 and the building was demolished. The picture is also marked by a lack of cars.

Richmond Station, 1955, was designed in an Art Deco style by J. Robb Scott for the Southern Railway in Portland Stone. The pre-war signs still advertise the Southern Electric and the London Midland and Scottish Railway which took over the North London Railway route. These companies had been nationalised in 1948 to form British Railways.

Richmond Station

Richmond Station was really two stations, the Old and New joined together. Work began on joining them during November 1935. A new building of steel-framed brick with Portland stone facing, a car park and goods yard were built on the north side. The booking hall was linked by stairs down to the concourse behind the bays and by a concrete footbridge to the new 600 foot long Waterloo platforms. The new booking hall was opened on 1 August 1937 and the next day, August Bank Holiday, 204 trains arrived between 9.00am and 5.00pm and 80,000 tickets were collected.

At the Southern Railway's Annual General Meeting in 1938, Mr R. Holland Martin said, 'In our new stations such as Surbiton and Richmond we have endeavoured to provide cheerful, clean and business-like structures capable of dealing expeditiously with our ever-increasing traffic with comfort to the passenger, for we find that improved stations bring increased revenue'.

The Richmond Kinema (Odeon) opened in April 1930 with a 1500 seater auditorium in the style of a seventeenth-century house of a Spanish nobleman with halophane concealed lighting costing £10,000. It was designed by Leathart and Granger (now much altered inside) who also designed Whitgift School buildings. It was renamed the Premier in 1940 and sold to Odeon cinemas in 1944. (British Architectural Library, RIBA, London)

Richmond Cinemas

Richmond has had five cinemas. The first cinema was in the Assembly Rooms in 1910 and called the Castle Electric Theatre. The second, third and fourth were eventually sold to Odeon. The Talbot Picture Theatre, Hill Street with an auditorium in green and blue opened in March 1911 but closed in April 1930 when the Richmond Kinema opened. The New Royalty Kinema (1000 seats) opened in 1914 and was converted from an eighteenth-century house. It was sold to Odeon in 1944 and Gaumont in 1949 and closed in 1980. The Richmond Kinema (Odeon), shown above, opened in April 1930 and is the only surviving cinema in Richmond. The fifth and final cinema was The Ritz, Sheen Road opened in May 1938 (2000 seats and a Wurlitzer) but it went bust and was sold to ABC in 1960. It was closed in December 1971 and demolished in the eighties and offices were built on the site, now Spencer House.

Kew Gardens Station, c. 1958, with a steam special to Richmond consisting of an ex-London Brighton and South Coast Railway two-coach push-pull set no. 717 and a steam engine pushing from behind. The kiosk on the right is now occupied by a cab firm. (Lens of Sutton)

A gathering outside Kew Road Methodist church, c. 1948. The foundation stone was laid on 11 October 1871 by Mr Foster-Newton and relaid in the building pictured on 20 March 1937 by Miss Foster-Newton.

The Coach and Horses Hotel, Kew Green, c. 1960, serving ales by Young & Co. On the left of it is Kew Green Garage offering complete overhauls and repairs and new and used cars as well as a petrol station. An Express Dairy milk float is outside, which took over deliveries from Hornby and Clarke.

Kew Green, c. 1960, where the Will Evans tea houses, the Imperial Restaurant and The Dieudonne (in the middle of the row of houses) have reverted to residential use. The pub sign is for the Rose and Crown